YOUR KNOWLEDGE HAS VALUE

- We will publish your bachelor's and master's thesis, essays and papers

- Your own eBook and book - sold worldwide in all relevant shops

- Earn money with each sale

Upload your text at www.GRIN.com and publish for free

Bibliographic information published by the German National Library:

The German National Library lists this publication in the National Bibliography; detailed bibliographic data are available on the Internet at http://dnb.dnb.de .

This book is copyright material and must not be copied, reproduced, transferred, distributed, leased, licensed or publicly performed or used in any way except as specifically permitted in writing by the publishers, as allowed under the terms and conditions under which it was purchased or as strictly permitted by applicable copyright law. Any unauthorized distribution or use of this text may be a direct infringement of the author s and publisher s rights and those responsible may be liable in law accordingly.

Imprint:

Copyright © 2018 GRIN Verlag
Print and binding: Books on Demand GmbH, Norderstedt Germany
ISBN: 9783668723849

This book at GRIN:

https://www.grin.com/document/428836

Caroline Mutuku

Comparative Analysis of the Educational Systems of the United States of America and Finland

GRIN Verlag

GRIN - Your knowledge has value

Since its foundation in 1998, GRIN has specialized in publishing academic texts by students, college teachers and other academics as e-book and printed book. The website www.grin.com is an ideal platform for presenting term papers, final papers, scientific essays, dissertations and specialist books.

Visit us on the internet:

http://www.grin.com/

http://www.facebook.com/grincom

http://www.twitter.com/grin_com

A comparison of the education disparity in the United States of America and the unified education system in Finland helps to underscore the differences in learning outcomes in various countries. Although Finland is a smaller economy, its education system consistently puts the learning outcomes higher than the United States of America. The overall availability of quality schools programs tend to be well established in wealthy industrialized nations than in the more poor developing ones (Childress, 2010). However, there are large differences that distinguish even countries that are geographically near each other and operating at similar economic development. For instance, all children aged three years are enrolled in an education program in Finland and France compared with twenty-eight percent of Spanish and Portuguese preschool children. Even within the same nation, access to education is more prevalent in urban centres compared with the rural areas. It is only in the last few decades that systematic research begun to look at the linkages that exist between national policy, childhood education programs, and the outcomes of the children (Sahlberg, 2012). There is widespread body of evidence that suggest that participation in a preschool program enhances cognitive development among children and prepares for success in their schooling.

The American education system is divided into Primary or elementary school, the upper primary or lower secondary school, and secondary school or high school. These schools are managed by the Local District Education Board (Childress, 2010). The primary school is composed of grade one to grade six; the upper primary takes grade seven and eight, while high school is made up of grades nine to twelve. The school staffs are composed of the headmaster, teachers and teachers' assistants, administration staff, counsellors, school nurse and custodial staff (Department of Education, 2008). Within a school district, the education policies are the same, however, education policies may vary from one district to another or from state to another, each state is in charge of the education system and they set the regulations on curriculum development although the management of curriculum and education policies tend to vary from one state or another (Wentzel, 2008).

Additionally, there are private schools in the United States of America. The private institutions are governed by the School Board of Trustees. The funding of the schools comes from their sponsors since they do not get any finance from the state or federal government (Corsi-Bunker, n. d.). The private schools are allowed to develop their academic and curriculum policies; however, many schools prefer to keep their policies in line with the recommendation of the Local Distract Education Boards. Together with the private schools there are the magnet schools, charter schools as well as homeschooling. The charter schools are public schools but started by parents or community organization to meet some specific educational needs such as serving minority populations or follow some special curriculum (Childress, 2010). The charter type of schools get funding from the state or the federal government but have the authority to operate independent of the Local District Education Board. They are called charter schools because they operate on a charter that delineate their mission and the programs they want to run as well as the size of the students' population. The charters are renewed after the agreed time elapses. Magnet schools, on the other hand, are special public schools with special interests and different method of instructions and are allowed to enrol students from across the United States of America (Sahlberg, 2012). These schools purpose is to avail unique education opportunities to those who could miss out on education, especially the minority groups. There is also the unique homeschooling which has always been recognized within the United States of America education system. The system employs tutors to teach students at their homes. The state provides the essential materials for homeschooling and on successful completion of the studies the home schooled students are recognized as having attained high school level of certification.

The management of the education system in the United States is governed by a variety of regulations that operate at the federal, state and the individual institutions levels. The federal government does not play an active role in the management of education since the management is the mandate of the Local District Education Board. However, it has the mandate to promote education reforms and policies at the national level. The federal government also oversees the schools funding programs as appropriated by Congress (Childress, 2010).

A distinct characteristic of the United States of America educational system is the powers given to the individual districts and institutions. The institutions chose the pedagogic methodology of instructions that best suits them (under the supervision of the district board). The outcome of the schools independence is the production of graduates with different exposure. The method creates some difficulties because of the different exposure to the educational curricula and materials that are supposed to satisfy the educational outcomes of a given level of education (Griffith & Kritsonis, 2007). Hence, the system creates an educational disparity and inconsistency in the overall educational outcome. It is a unique approach to educational management that is only practised in the United States of America (Sahlberg, 2012).

The United States of America education system is contrasted with the education of a small European nation-state called Finland. The reason for this comparison is because in an international assessment on educational outcomes for over thirty countries which included Finland and the United States of America undertaken by programme for International Student Assessment (PISA) the finish students had the highest scores, and therefore, Finland may be said to have the best educational system (OECD, 2012). Thus, in order to discover if that is the case, a comparison of the two nation's educational systems is moot.

In Finland, the children start primary school when they are six years old after going through the preschool education system International Association of Universities, 2006. The students have to complete a nine-year basic education after which they can opt to proceed to the general upper secondary school or join a vocational high school (Sahlberg, 2012). The general secondary school education leads to the matriculation examination and on passing a student can proceed to a tertiary institution. The vocational schools are allowed to offer a kind of Vocational upper secondary education. The students attain a vocational qualification after three years (Childress, 2010). The qualification allows the students to access the tertiary institutions, however, should the student chose to further his education through the vocational system he can pursue a specialist vocational qualification. However, the specialist vocational qualification is mostly targeted at employed adults and is typically a competence-based qualification. The difference with the United States of America education system is the opportunities to prepare for higher learning after the primary school either through the general secondary schools or through the vocational secondary schools (Sahlberg, 2012). The vocational secondary school allows the student to pursue a trade while the general secondary allows for the academic pursuit. However, both systems qualifications allow the students who pass well to pursue higher education at a tertiary institution of their choice.

Unlike the United States of America, the Finnish education system is centralised, and governed through the state's policies. The finish government, through the education reform of the 1960s and 1970s, made primary education compulsory. The administration of education, policy formulation, and execution are done by the National Board of Education (NBE) (Sahlberg, 2012). However, the success of the basic education was not followed by the secondary school since a change in the political climate shifted towards the more decentralised system which gradually allowed municipality to have a measure of control of the curricula development although the common national curricula was the guiding force behind the education reform (Koskenniemi, 2012).

The idea of comprehensive education system emerged as part of a larger social discourse in the 1960s as Finland struggled to establish social and economic equality. Consequently, the Finish education system is embedded in a society with established social safety networks and a broad commitment to a healthy development of children. Thus, the education system in Finland emphasise equity and well-being of the students and rely on the concept of inclusive education. Preschool education is optional, but it is available as from the age of six

(Koskenniemi, 2012). About ninety-eight percent of preschool age children go to school. Most of the schools, primary secondary, and college, are funded by the state and, therefore, private schools (which are common in the United States of America) do not exist in Finland. Finland spends close to six percent of its GDP on education (Childress, 2010).

Education opportunities and, consequently, good learning outcomes are available across the nation. After the state abolished streaming in comprehensive schools at the turn of the 1980s decade, the learning expectations were made the same for all children and the achievement gap between the high and low achievers was narrowed (Sahlberg, 2012). Thus, all children, regardless of their interests and abilities had to study sciences, mathematics, and foreign languages in the same classes. Before the education reform in mid-1980, the students were streamed into three levels according to their abilities and performance on a particular subject. The evidence of the equitable student outcomes was established in 2000 through the Programme for International Student Achievement study. In the survey, Finland came out with the smallest performance variance between schools in reading literacy within the OECD (OECD, 2012).

The education reform looked at through an international perspective is based on institutional structures that were put in place in the 1980s (Koskenniemi, 2012). Consequently, the changes in education after 1990 focused on innovations rather than the establishment of institutional structures except in the establishment of the new polytechnic system. The education policies are heavily intertwined with the social, economic, and political policies and culture (Government of Finland, 2010). Education in Finland is treated as a public good whose contribution to the well-being of all is paramount especially in nation building. Consequently, the liberal approach to education has contributed tremendously to the well-performing knowledge economy and good governance (Koskenniemi, 2012).

The difference between the education policies adopted by the United States of America, through the No Child Left Behind Act and Finland Basic Education Act is exemplified through the titles of the Acts. The United States of America Act refers to the disparities obtaining within the education system while the Finland education policy is anchored on equity within the state's education system (Sahlberg, 2012). While the No Child Left Behind policies focus on the funds to be availed to education institutions in the effort to close the gaps between low and high achievers, the Basic Education Act focuses on the entire education system, with emphasis on education for all, irrespective of the economic situation of the parents (Government of Finland, 2010). Thus, the United States of America education policies are driven by the disparities of the political system while the Finland education system is anchored on the provision of learning opportunities for all and the building of a cohesive society (OECD, 2012).

A comparison of the students' population can shed light on the education disparity in the United States of America and the near uniformity of the Finland education system. By 2009, the students' population stood at fifty million, ranging from preschool to high school, while Finland had five hundred and sixty thousand students in the same grade range (OECD, 2008).. Thus, the United States of America students' population was one hundred times that of Finland. The students' population in the United States of America is composed of different ethnic groups, perhaps, the reason that could explain the need for the various types of schools found in the country. In 2007, whites made fifty-five percent of the students' population; seventeen percent were African American, the remaining thirty percent were drawn from Hispanic, Asian and Pacific Islanders. On the other hand, Finland had only two percent of the students' population who were not Finnish. Consequently, Finland can afford to have a homogenous education policy while the United States cannot. The Finland government funds all educational activities and programs equally, while the United States of America funds the public educational institutions disproportionally (Lastra-Anadón & Peterson, 2012).

Another unique characteristic of the Finnish education system is that the basic education teachers have Masters Degrees and can teach all subjects except for foreign languages (Fritz, 2014). Every school has a special support team of professionals that classroom teachers can seek help from with pedagogy issues. The teams also have a nurse, a special educator, general trustee and a psychologist (Government of Finland, 2010). The special team handles the needs of the students who learning challenges. On the other hand, eight percent of the teachers in the United States of America do not have a Bachelors Degree. The United States of America education system does not operate a national curriculum, a situation that complicates the students learning outcomes (Gamerman, 2008). The education management is determined by the Tenth Amendment, which declares that each state should be responsible for the development and execution of the education curriculum. Suffice to say, there are about fifty different education curriculum in the country compared to only one unified curriculum in Finland (Clack, 2007). Whereas the United States of America educational system relies on formal assessment Finland has a liberal assessment system that does not overly rely on examinations to determine which student moves to the next level.

To sum up, a comparison of the education system in the United States of America and Finland helps to underscore the differences in learning outcomes in various countries. Finland is a small economy compared to the United States of America; however, its education system consistently posts better educational outcomes than the United States of America. The overall availability of quality schools programs in Finland tends to allow for better educational development of the students than is the case in the United States of America. Finland has also invested heavily in the development of education, because it is a homogeneous country, the administration of a common curriculum is made easy.

References

Childress, D. (2010). *Education in the United States and Finland: A Comparative Analysis.* Retrieved from:
http://www.nacfam.org/Portals/0/Workforce/21stCLS_WhitePaper_12-3-08.pdf

Clack, G. (2007). A Diverse Educational System: Structure, Standards, and Challenges. *Americas studies Journal*, 49, 10-23.

Corsi-Bunker, A. (n.d.). *Guide to the Education system in the United States.* Retrieved from: http://www.isss.umn.edu/publications/USEducation/2.pdf

Department of Education. (2008). USNEI: Organization of U.S. Education. Retrieved from disparities: An unexpected consequence for the commonwealth of Virginia. *Journal of Education Finance, 33*(3), 238-261.

Fritz, G. (2014). *Finland has secret for great schools: Great teachers.* Retrieved from: http://www.providencejournal.com/opinion/commentary/20140829-gregory-k.-fritz-finland-has-secret-for-great-schools-great-teachers.ece

Gamerman, E. (2008). *What Makes Finnish Kids So Smart?* Retrieved from: HTTP://ONLINE.WSJ.COM/ARTICLES/SB120425355065601997

Government of Finland. (2010). *General education in Finland. Ministry of Education and Culture.* Retrieved from:
http://www.minedu.fi/OPM/Koulutus/koulutusjaerjesteland=en

Griffith, K., & Kritsonis, W. (2007). The achievement gap between African-American and non-minority students: How can we close the gap? *The Lamar University Journal of Student Research*, 1-5.
http://www.aurora.edu/documents/academics/specialprograms/honors/Deanna%20C.%20Childress%20%20Education%20in%20the%20United%20States%20and%20Finland.pdf

Koskenniemi, M. (2012). The New Teacher Education System in Finland. *International Review of Education, 18*(1), 212-216.

Lastra-Anadón, C., & Peterson, P. (2012). What U.S. schools can and cannot learn from other countries. *Education Next, 12*(1), 53-59.

OECD. (2008). *What Makes Schools System Perform: Seeing School Systems through the Prism of PISA.* Retrieved from:
http://www.oecd.org/education/school/programmeforinternationalstudentassessmentpisa/33858946.pdf

OECD. (2012). *Programme for International Student Assessment (PISA) Results from PISA 2012*. Retrieved from: http://www.oecd.org/unitedstates/PISA-2012-results-US.pdf

Sahlberg, P. (2012). *Finland Shows Us What Equal opportunity Looks Like*. Retrieved from: http://www.cimo.fi/instancedata/prime_product_julkaisu/cimo/embeds/cimowwwstructure/25534_American_educator_spring2012.pdf

Wentzel, F. (2008). *American 21st Century Learning System*. Retrieved from: http://www2.ed.gov/about/offices/list/ous/international/usnei/us/edlite-org-us.html

YOUR KNOWLEDGE HAS VALUE

- We will publish your bachelor's and master's thesis, essays and papers

- Your own eBook and book - sold worldwide in all relevant shops

- Earn money with each sale

Upload your text at www.GRIN.com and publish for free